Three nationwide radio networks broadcasted this song, dedicated to Franklin D. Roosevelt. Cover of sheet music. *Courtesy of the National Park Service.*

Published by The History Press
Charleston, SC 29403
www.historypress.net

All photographs are courtesy of the National Archives unless otherwise noted.

First published 2009

Manufactured in the United States

ISBN 978.1.59629.729.6

Library of Congress Cataloging-in-Publication Data

Huddleston, Connie M.
Kentucky's Civilian Conservation Corps / Connie Huddleston.
p. cm.
Includes bibliographical references and index.
ISBN 978-1-59629-729-6 (alk. paper)
1. Civilian Conservation Corps (U.S.) 2. Forests and forestry--Kentucky--History--
20th century. 3. Parks--Kentucky--History--20th century. I. Title.

SD144.K4H83 2009
333.76'1509769--dc22
2009030603

KENTUCKY'S
CIVILIAN
CONSERVATION
CORPS

CONNIE M. HUDDLESTON

Charleston   London

THE
History
PRESS

THE CCC — A YO

to work

— and to conserv

Across the nation, recruiting posters for the CCC enticed young men to join the corps. Most enrollees tell of hearing about the CCC from other local enrollees.

G MAN'S OPPORTUNITY

to live
to learn
to build

our National Resources

Contents

Acknowledgements

My fascination with the Civilian Conservation Corps (CCC) started with a series of exhibits I planned for Georgia State Parks. It grew with the discovery of hundreds of CCC photographs at the National Archives in College Park, Maryland. Later, the stories of these boys and young men who created so many of our national and state parks captured my complete attention and enticed me to write about the CCC for the people of Georgia, where I currently live, and Kentucky, which will always be my home. This book is dedicated to those "CCC boys" whose faces look out from these historic photographs, telling us of a time when a president promised a "New Deal" for all Americans and made good on his promise to many young men by creating the CCC.

Books may be authored by one individual, but they always seem to be a group effort. My support group deserves and receives my sincere thanks. First, I thank Charlie, my husband, for encouraging my efforts in all that I do. He is also valued as an editor. Second, I thank my mother, Carol Aldridge, whose unwavering love and support has always been there. Next, I thank two friends who served as personal editors. First is Sherron Lawson, without whom I cannot imagine my world. She is a great editor but an even better f... Finally, there is Gwen Koehler, daughter of a CCC mar... some of her precious time and talents to edit both of m...

I also give my special thanks to Lori and J.O. Powers ... and photographs of Fred Powers, one of Kentucky's CC... would not have been possible without the great stories ... Kentucky's CCC boys.

My editor, John Wilkinson, made this project easier t... by giving me lots of advice and quickly answering my m... I appreciate his efforts on my behalf to see this book publ... History Press.

Introduction

It has frequently been said that someone, or some group, made a "significant contribution" to his fellow man, the environment or society as a whole. Journalists and historians have often applied this same catchphrase to the Civilian Conservation Corps (CCC), the most popular of President Franklin D. Roosevelt's New Deal programs implemented to relieve the substantial burdens placed on every American during the Great Depression. The CCC planted trees; provided soil conservation measures; built trails, firebreaks, fire towers, bridges and state and national parks; and supplied labor for other necessary jobs, all while leaving a legacy of far-reaching impact on the American landscape. Yet few Americans today realize that the most significant role played by the CCC was the employment, education and enrichment FDR's forest army provided to a lost generation of young men.

In the summer of 1932, the Democratic Party nominated Franklin D. Roosevelt, then governor of New York, for president. In his acceptance speech, Roosevelt focused on the problems created by the Great Depression, telling the American people, "I pledge you, I pledge myself, to a new deal for the American people." FDR took the oath of office on March 4, 1933, and faced a nation in which soup lines fed many of the 12 to 15 million unemployed. Eleven thousand of the United States' twenty-five thousand banks had failed, robbing millions of Americans of their uninsured savings. Since Black Tuesday—October 29, 1929—trade had plummeted, construction had halted and the mining and logging industries had collapsed. Manufacturing had fallen to only 54 percent of its early 1929 level. Across the southern plains, the Great Dust Bowl had emerged, turning to dust farmlands devastated by poor agricultural practices and years of sustained drought. Crops failed, the sky darkened with blowing dust and even more Americans suffered the reality of the Great Depression. One in four young men between the ages of fifteen and

Many saw Franklin Delano Roosevelt's love of nature and the outdoor life as a contributing factor to his establishment of the Civilian Conservation Corps. *Courtesy of the Library of Congress.*

twenty-four found himself unemployed, undereducated and living in poverty. Many took to the roads and rails, moving from town to town in search of food and work. They became known as "the teenage tramps of America."

Only five days into his administration, Roosevelt presented his plan to employ America's young, unmarried men, ages eighteen to twenty-five, in conservation programs across the states. On March 9, 1933, he outlined the program's basic concepts to his secretaries of agriculture, the interior and war, the director of the budget, the army's judge advocate-general and the solicitor of the Department of the Interior. He demanded immediate action, asking Colonel Kyle Rucker, the army's judge advocate-general, and Edward Finney, the interior solicitor, to prepare a draft bill by that evening. It was completed and presented to the president at 9:00 p.m.

They proposed hiring 500,000 young men a year to be employed in conservation and public work projects. In an ambitious plan, FDR wanted 250,000 young men employed by early summer. The plan called for several agencies to play roles in the program's development. The army would recruit the enrollees and organize the camps. The Departments of Agriculture and the Interior would create and run the work programs.

Introduction

In his third press conference, on March 15, 1933, FDR expounded on his ideas about creating work in America's forests, the number of men that could be employed and the proposed wage of one dollar per day. Initially, there was opposition from organized labor to the low wage to be paid (average wage at that time was eighteen dollars per week for men) and from the public about the army's role in the program. In support of the program, which organized labor said would create "open air sweat shops," Secretary of Labor Frances Perkins emphasized the administration's view of this new program as a relief measure directed at one segment of society: young, unmarried men who would be provided with food, shelter and clothing, along with medical and dental care. These young men would be volunteers, not drafted. Ms. Perkins defended the army's role as necessary to create the organization and infrastructure needed by the corps.

Roosevelt's message to Congress on March 21 read:

> *I propose to create a Civilian Conservation Corps to be used in simple work, not interfering with normal employment, and confining itself to forestry, the prevention of soil erosion, flood control, and similar projects…More importantly, however, than the material gains, will be the moral and spiritual value of such work. The overwhelming majority of unemployed Americans, who are now walking the streets and receiving private or public relief, would infinitely prefer to work. We can take a vast army of these unemployed out into healthful surroundings. We can eliminate to some extent at least the threat that enforced idleness brings to spiritual and moral stability. It is not a panacea for all the unemployment, but it is an essential step in this emergency…I estimate that 250,000 men can be given temporary employment by early summer if you will give me the authority to proceed within the next two weeks.*

Congress passed the Emergency Conservation Act on March 27. On March 31, FDR signed the bill. On April 17, the first camp, Camp Roosevelt, opened in Virginia. On April 27, national news stories reported that 25,000 men were already enrolled and 35,000 more were authorized. By the first of July, some 275,000 enrollees were employed in thirteen hundred camps spread across our nation.

FDR chose Robert Fechner, a highly touted labor leader, to head the CCC. Fechner's excellent standing with the unions helped settle the controversy over wages, and his experienced, hands-on leadership style provided the strong start desired by the president. Born in Chattanooga, Tennessee, and raised in Georgia, Fechner dropped out of school at age sixteen to sell candy and newspapers on Georgia trains before becoming a machinist's apprentice for the Georgia Central Railroad. Fechner continued to be the common man in government, picturing himself as a "potato bug amongst dragonflies" who often proclaimed that his clerks were better educated than he. Fechner lived in a modestly priced hotel room when in Washington, D.C., although he could often be found traveling around the nation, visiting the various CCC camps. Fechner chose James J. McEntee as his assistant director. These two men ran the CCC until its abolishment in 1942.

Robert Fechner served as director of the CCC from its inception until his death in 1939. Fechner, who knew little about conservation, was a good organizer and administrator, with a sense of fairness, tact and patience. He was photographed here visiting a CCC camp.

The CCC consisted of nine administrative regions or corps, each with its own headquarters. Each corps was divided into districts. The first number of three-digit company numbers and the second number of four-digit company numbers designate which corps trained and organized the company. All Kentucky-based companies were trained in Fifth Corps. *Author's personal collection.*

By late May, Kentucky newspapers reported the number of CCC recruits from each area and provided details of their training and deployment to camps. The *Middlesboro Daily News* reported on May 22:

> *Eighty-one young men, forty-one of them furnished by the Middlesboro district and forty by the Pineville district, have been accepted by the Welfare Officers for the forestry work…the Army Recruiting Office in Middlesboro is already receiving young men from all over eastern Kentucky for examination and transportation to Camp Knox.*

The article detailed the number of recruits from each area and announced the first camps to be established at Mammoth Cave and Cumberland Falls.

From its start in 1933 until after the outbreak of World War II, the Civilian Conservation Corps enrolled approximately 2.5 million men, including World War I veterans, Native Americans and some 200,000 African Americans. After arriving underweight, malnourished and uneducated, most recruits left the corps in good health and with at least a high school diploma. A few received college degrees.

Life in the CCC

W. Francis Persons served as chief of the CCC selection process under the Department of Labor. Local officials tasked with enrolling young men for the program chose those from the neediest families first, using welfare and unemployment rolls. Enrollees encompassed a wide range of the population as boys and young men from cities, villages and farms agreed to a six-month enlistment. Many had never seen a forest, been away from home overnight or earned a wage. Early numbers showed that only 45 percent of enrollees had ever been employed before joining the CCC, and only 13 percent had graduated from high school.

Enrollees signed their enlistment papers and were often transported directly to an army training facility. Here they received a complete physical, including inoculations, followed by two weeks of conditioning training. The army issued each enrollee two uniforms: a denim work uniform and a formal uniform. Many former CCC boys will tell you that those uniforms were "real nice" and attracted the attention of the local girls. The boys also received long johns, which one Kentucky recruit noted was the first underwear he had ever worn. Their newly issued shaving kit with toiletry items also created moments of mirth, as some of the boys had never used a toothbrush and paste.

Initially, CCC-issued uniforms came from army stockpiles. Once this source was depleted, CCC funds were used to purchase uniforms designed for the CCC. A glance at many CCC photographs will illustrate variations of uniforms within individual camps. Dress uniforms from army stockpiles were altered for the wearer and modified to look "less military." But "CCC fit," meaning either way too large or too small, continued to be the term used by the boys when discussing their uniform woes.

Each month, enrollees received five dollars of their thirty-dollar pay in vouchers, and the remainder was sent to their families or, if none existed, placed in a savings account. With housing and meals provided, most enrollees found their five-dollar allotment sufficient for their needs. Many CCC enrollees have commented that this money was "a necessity" at home and their main reason for joining the corps.

In Kentucky, CCC boys received their in-processing and conditioning training at Fort Knox. Early CCC enrollment in 1933 brought twenty-five hundred men to Fort Knox on May 30; the largest number to arrive on any one day. During the first week of June that year, fourteen thousand men camped at Fort Knox as they received their conditioning training. The army used every tent it could locate to house these enrollees and called into service field kitchens to prepare meals. Special trains arrived at Knox and were loaded first with supplies for the camps, including full field kitchens, tents and administrative materials, and then with companies of two hundred men before they were sent out to newly established camps.

Earl L. Paul wrote of his experience during those first days at the fort: "We were lined up in single file, issued our dog tags, and mess kits, and then led to chow. What a hungry mob!" Earl also wrote of signing his name so

Aerial view of the CCC training center at Fort Knox, Kentucky.

many times that first day that "were we given five cents for each signature, we would never [have] had to sign at all." He told of sleeping on an iron cot with a straw tick, which he filled himself from the stable, no pillow and two army wool blankets.

During their stay at Fort Knox, all enrollees received first-aid training, which included treatment of wounds, snakebite and sunstroke. They participated in physical training exercises such as calisthenics and learned to march in columns of three, as the army didn't want the boys to look like army units, which drilled in columns of four. During the initial buildup of the CCC, many who arrived at Fort Knox found themselves helping to build the facilities needed for the expected influx of CCC recruits.

The army assigned officers to each camp to handle day-to-day operations. To meet this expanded need for peacetime officers, the army called up reserve officers and offered early graduation at its military academies. The CCC then expanded its offer to include marine and navy officers. Additionally, army doctors and dentists served at each camp or moved from camp to camp as needed within a district. Each camp also had a project supervisor, who was chosen based on the camp's work tasks. He directed the daily work. Vital to the success of each camp were the "local experienced men," or LEMs. Usually eight per camp, these men provided training for the young enrollees, and in exchange, the CCC furnished much-needed employment for local men and added more money to the local economy. LEMs were paid the civil service pay rate for their particular skills.

As the enrollees left the army training centers, they were assigned to companies of two hundred men. These companies served as a unit. Many Kentucky enrollees found themselves assigned to companies bound for distant states, such as Idaho, Montana, California and Oregon. An enrollee could reenlist for another six months at the end of his initial enlistment. At this time, he could request a company closer to home; however, many stayed with their initial companies for subsequent enlistments.

Camps were either junior or veteran (former Spanish-American War and World War I soldiers) and white or "colored." Camps were most often segregated after the failure of Kentucky's initial experiment to place several African American enrollees in each camp to perform menial tasks such as food preparation.

The camp's mess hall served three hot meals a day. As many enrollees arrived undernourished and underweight, few complained about the chow. As a result of the nutritious food and hard work, most CCC boys gained from eight to fourteen pounds and about a half inch in height during their enlistments.

Official company photograph taken at Fort Knox in 1934. Three army training officers are pictured in the first row. *Author's personal collection.*

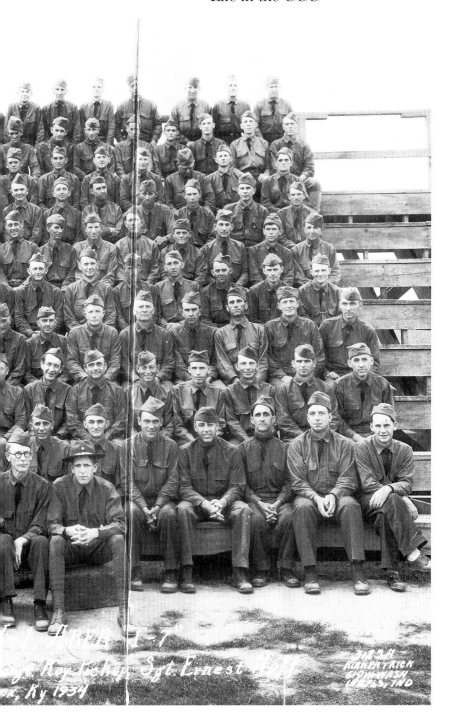

CCC camps were built following guidelines prepared by the Department of Agriculture. Pictured is Camp Cromwell at Henderson, occupied by Company 1540.

By October 1935, Kentucky had opened thirty-five camps. As new camps were established, the enrollees lived in surplus army tents while building their barracks, mess halls, latrines and other necessary buildings. Most camps followed the same plan, in which a parade field was a prominent feature. In subsequent years, the CCC developed a set of prefab buildings that could be transported to new camps.

Each camp also followed a strict daily schedule that began at 6:00 a.m. and ended at 9:00 p.m. This daily routine and army-style discipline established a sense of unit pride and comradery among the enrollees. While this military-style life led many civilians to believe that their young men were being trained for military service, most CCC boys realized that the strict schedule and discipline were necessary.

Kentucky newspapers often carried stories of the CCC's arrival in an area. At Harlin, "barefooted wide-eyed mountain gals, who looked shying from under their bonnets," welcomed Company 512, made up entirely of Kentucky mountain boys. They arrived by train and then marched to their new camp. These same boys bragged about the camp's "18-holer." In that same June 12, 1933 edition of the *Middlesboro Daily News*, another article told of the CCC's official newspaper, *Happy Days*, which printed its first issue on May 20, and about Company 512's one-page news sheet edited by mountain boy Lonze Rousch.

Communities often kept a close watch on their homes, livestock and daughters when the CCC first arrived, as CCC boys were heralded as

Life in the CCC

Reveille sounded at 6:00 a.m., calling the men to the day. Physical training began at 6:30 a.m. in most camps, followed by breakfast and the day's work.

Wooden barracks housed the men at each camp. Most were heated by wood or coal-burning stoves, and many had electricity. Fred Powers took this snapshot of the inside of Barracks 4, Company 592, at General Butler State Park. *Courtesy of Fred Powers's family.*

Perhaps the most important building was the camp's mess hall, often run by an army-trained cook. Some enrollees were also assigned as cooks rather than working on the camp's project. Fred Powers served as cook at General Butler State Park. This photo graced the front of a postcard that the men could send home to their families. *Courtesy of Fred Powers's family.*

Life in the CCC

In 1938, at FDR's insistence, a new dress uniform was created for the CCC. The old (left) and new uniforms are shown here. The Department of the Navy designed the new uniform.

Often, the army assigned reserve officers to the camps. The men pictured are (from left) Captain G.A. Norris, Captain J.L. Adams, Lieutenant P.L. Williams and Lieutenant William Schoenburger. They were assigned to Manchester, Gooserock and Bell Farm.

Dated July 31, 1936, this photograph is of the technical personnel at Natural Bridge. Pictured from left to right are O.D. Rose, Howard Robinson, Charles Marshall Jr., A.M. Peterson, T.G. Strunk, R.H. Gunter (project superintendent), G.A. Mountjoy and J.C. Brandenburgh.

"urban scum." Usually within a few weeks, the locals began welcoming the hardworking boys and expressed their gratitude for the positive impact on the local community's economy.

The workday ended at 4:00 p.m., giving the men a few hours of free time each day before "retreat," when the flags were lowered and the evening meal was served. This free time gave the men a chance to carry out personal chores, attend classes and participate in sports or other activities. Weekends were generally free time, unless inclement weather had kept the men from their work during the week. Enrollees could leave camp and visit home if it was nearby or make a trip into the local town. Company trucks loaded with CCC boys often made a Saturday trip into town for organized jaunts to the local movie house, a sporting event or a community dance.

Hardworking enrollees could earn extra money by being advanced to assistant leader or leader. Assistant leaders received thirty-six dollars per month, while leaders received forty-five dollars. Corps enrollee leaders were allowed to keep the extra pay instead of sending it home to their families.

The CCC's Conservation Mission in Kentucky

While many know of the CCC's work in our nation's forests, this was not the CCC's only mission. Each state found specific projects for its camps that included such tasks as building dams, constructing irrigation systems or repairing historical structures.

In Kentucky, fifteen camps in the Cumberland National Forest were devoted almost entirely to forestry work (see Table 1). Other camps carried out forestry work on private or state lands. Unfortunately, few photographs of CCC workers carrying out forestry projects in Kentucky exist at the National Archives. However, CCC official photographers, including Walter Mead, captured forestry work images all across the nation suitable for CCC publicity.

TABLE 1. CUMBERLAND NATIONAL FOREST CCC CAMPS

CAMP	COMPANY	COUNTY	POST OFFICE	DATES ACTIVE
F-1	1559	Wolfe	Pine Ridge	Summer '33–Summer '35
F-2	1502	Jackson	McKee	Winter '33/'34–Summer '36
F-3	564	Jackson	McKee	Winter '33/'34–Winter '37/'38
F-4	578	Rowan	Clearfield/Morehead	Winter '33/'34–Summer '41
F-5	3544	Laurel	London	Summer '35–unknown
F-6	523	McCreary	Greenwood	Winter '33/'34–Summer '36
F-7	509	Whitley	Williamsburg	Summer '35–Winter '37/'38
F-8	1539	Menifee	Frenchburg	Winter '34/'35–Winter '37/'38
F-9	1559	Powell	Stanton/Bowen	Summer '35–Summer '42
F-10	3546	Lee	Beattyville	Summer '35–Summer '36
F-11	3552	Laurel	London	Summer '35–Winter '38/'39
F-12	1502	McCreary	Sterns	Winter '35/'36–Summer '42
F-13	564	Jackson	McKee	Winter '37/'38–Summer '42
F-14	509	McCreary	Bell Farm	Summer '38–Summer '42
F-15	3552	Laurel	London	Winter '38/'39–Winter '41/'42

CCC workers heading into a newly forested area were captured on film by Walter Mead in one of a series of CCC publicity shots.

As the CCC boys quickly learned how to cut diseased and dead trees, clear undergrowth, harvest seeds and seedlings and fight forest fires, the nation and the press dubbed the corps "Roosevelt's Tree Army." Camps were established as near to the work project as possible so that little time was lost on transportation each day. Sometimes side camps were established near small project areas. These side camps often had their own temporary mess halls and related facilities, although they employed only a portion of the camp's company. Side camps frequently had no permanent buildings, and the boys slept in tents. President Roosevelt had specified that side camps would contain no more than twenty enrollees, be limited to a specific task, return to home camp for weekends and be under the control of forestry personnel.

Tales from national forest CCC camps abound with wildlife encounters, cutting trails through mountains using dynamite and never-ending, backbreaking labor. The camp at Gooserock built a footpath aptly called Rattlesnake Bluff, so named for an area so full of rattlesnakes that locals avoided that neck of the woods. These selfsame boys also spent some extra time on weekends building one trail that created a shortcut to the mess hall,

The CCC's Conservation Mission in Kentucky

Working in pairs, CCC boys planted trees in areas to be reforested. A good team could set six hundred or more seedlings each day.

This famous CCC photograph shows a young enrollee, who has shed his work shirt, planting seedlings beneath a hot sun. Photographs such as this appeared in newspapers and recruiting advertisements across the United States.

since taking the trail around the mountain meant that "all the baloney was gone" by the time they arrived for lunch!

Soil conservation camps worked mostly on private lands under such agencies as the Bureau of Reclamation, the Bureau of Land Management and the Soil Conservation Service (SCS). The SCS used CCC labor to demonstrate soil conservation efforts to owners of desolated farmland across the nation. Many days were spent working on such measures on private farms. Personnel from state agencies and land grant colleges actually operated the camps and followed guidelines that initially limited the work to "controlling gullies by means of soil-saving dams, forest planting and vegetation."

Work was carried out in all types of weather. The enrollees received heavy winter gear, including gloves, coats and lined work boots. Here, CCC men plant trees on a recently cleared roadside slope at Natural Bridge.

The CCC's Conservation Mission in Kentucky

Forestry work often included the clearing of firebreaks, trails and mountain roads. This photo from Natural Bridge captures the boys clearing a forest trail.

The book *We Can Take It* quoted one CCC enrollee as saying, "If the CCC does nothing more than impress upon us the love for nature, it will be a success." Yet many CCC boys moaned about the work as they rolled into their cots each night. This comic is from *Hysterical History: Civilian Conservation Corps. Author's personal collection.*

The educational building at SCS-15 at Elizabethtown was one of the CCC's prefabricated buildings.

The CCC's Conservation Mission in Kentucky

Along with carrying out soil conservation tasks, Company 1515 learned agricultural engineering and mapmaking from the LEMs and educational personnel at SCS-15.

Cecil L. Wohlwinder served with Company 3563 at Carlisle and told of moving rocks from fields to make them tillable. His company also cleared water gaps so that marshy areas could drain. He claimed that every time he moved a rock, he saw a snake. The company used freshly cut cedar trees to fill erosion ditches and chopped down locust trees for fence posts. Cecil remembers sack lunches that consisted of one bologna sandwich, one cheese sandwich and one "jam" sandwich, so named because you never knew what would be jammed between two slices of bread.

At Marion in Crittenden County, PE-59/SCS-9 planted over 120,000 black locusts and sixty-three bushels of black walnut seedlings. This veteran camp worked on private farms from May 1933 until November 1935 before the camp was closed.

As soil conservation work progressed, the SCS taught the use of terraces and contours and how to plant off-season and fallow-field cover crops. In Kentucky, twenty-five soil conservation camps worked exclusively on private lands. Camp designations sometimes changed as their tasks changed or the agency overseeing the camps changed. Appendix A lists the commonwealth's soil conservation, erosion and drainage camps.

Developing Kentucky's State Parks

Across the nation, the development of state and national parks emerged as the significant mission of the CCC. The creation of public parks corresponded closely to FDR's ideas of conservation, since most of the parks featured large forested tracts crisscrossed with hiking trails to scenic views, rental cabins, camping areas and outdoor recreation venues. Some states created their first parks under the guidance of the National Park Service using CCC labor. Others—like Kentucky, which established a parks department in 1924—used CCC labor and WPA funds to create and/or enhance their parks. Under the leadership of Dr. Willard Rouse Jillson, the commonwealth's first parks commissioner, Kentuckians witnessed the development or enhancement of nine state parks employing nine years of CCC labor.

TABLE 2. STATE PARKS DEVELOPED BY THE CCC

CAMP	COMPANY	NAME	COUNTY	POST OFFICE
SP-1	509	Cumberland Falls	Whitley/McCreary	Corbin
SP-2	567	Natural Bridge	Powell	Slade
SP-3	548	Pine Mountain	Bell	Pineville
SP-4	566	Levi Jackson	Laurel	London
SP-6	592	Butler Memorial	Carroll	Carrollton
SP-7	563	Cumberland Falls	Whitley	Williamsburg
SP-8	583	Columbus	Hickman	Columbus
SP-9/ASCA-2	1540	Audubon Memorial	Hickman	Henderson
SP-10	563	Pine Mountain	Bell	Pineville
SP-11[a, b]	unknown	Otter Creek	Meade	Rock Haven
SP-12[a, c]	3557	Dawson Springs	Hopkins	Dawson Springs

[a] No job-related photographs found in National Archives collection.

[b] Now owned by the City of Louisville and closed to the public.

[c] Now part of Pennyrile Forest State Park.

The Cumberland River falls 68 feet at the falls, which range from 125 to 300 feet in width, depending on the season. On moonlit nights, the thundering waters create one of only two known moonbows. The other can be seen at Victoria Falls in Africa.

On May 10, 1924, Dr. Jillson, a Kentucky historian and geologist, delivered his presidential address before the Kentucky Academy of Science. Speaking of Cumberland Falls, he eloquently stated, "A beauty spot in every sense of the word. Kentuckians should know more about and value more highly this majestic waterfall. It possesses now every attribute of a well chosen state park. The pity is that it is not one already." Further describing the area, Jillson added:

> An old rambling hotel which dates back to Civil War times and before is situated on the conglomerate shelf which holds up this waterfall, and affords a kindly oldtime southern hospitality for tourists who pass that way. The region offers much to the nature lover, the fisherman, the hunter or the mountain climber and would all things considered, be ideal as a State Park site. During the past fifty years thousands have visited or summered at this point and have come to love it for its restful natural beauty and ruggedness.

In 1927, the local Kiwanis Club sponsored the building of a trail from the town to the falls. Approximately two hundred volunteers worked for nine weeks to complete the trail. Later that year, Kentuckian Thomas Coleman du Pont offered to buy the 593-acre tract of land containing the falls and to donate it to the state as a park in order to prevent the building of a dam just above the falls by the Cumberland River Power Company. Du Pont, a Massachusetts Institute of Technology graduate, served in the United States Senate as a representative from Delaware after his retirement from business in Kentucky and Pennsylvania. Although du Pont died before the park became a reality, his widow purchased the land for $400,000 and donated it to the commonwealth. Kentuckians witnessed the dedication of the park on August 21, 1931. That same year, a highway was completed to the park, giving thousands of visitors a safe, paved route to the scenic site. The CCC began work at the site in the winter of 1933–34, when two camps were opened. SP-7 closed in the summer of 1935, while SP-1 remained open until the winter of 1937–38.

E.S. Shipp, U.S. Forest Service photographer, captured this view of the Cumberland Falls CCC camp from Highway 26 in August 1934. SP-1 furnished work for two CCC companies, 509 (shown here) near Corbin and 563 near Williamsburg.

This photograph of SP-1's CCC company area is dated 1934. Taken by Spencer A___koff of Detroit, its caption names the location of the camp as Williamsburg.

The Renfro family were the first permanent landowners to live near the waterfall, building a small cabin in 1850. Socrates Owens purchased the property in 1875 and built a hotel on the site. In 1902, Henry Brunson bought and renamed the inn the Brunson Inn. It was renamed Moonbow Inn in 1931. This photo was taken after landscaping had been completed by the CCC. The Moonbow Inn burned in 1949.

Williamsburg, Ky.

Excavation for the park's new lodge began in early 1934. The men used hand tools and manual labor for the excavation, as mechanized equipment was not made available.

CCC enrollees learned valuable construction skills while building the du Pont Lodge. Quarry work and/or masonry skills often helped former enrollees find civilian employment after their enlistment period.

The completed du Pont Lodge was a rambling twenty-six-room structure of stone and log. Hand-hewn timbers beamed across many of the open spaces, giving the lodge a rustic, yet majestic, feel. CCC men collected rock from all over the countryside to use at the park for foundations, chimneys, fireplaces, buildings and steps.

Interior photograph of the original du Pont Lodge.

A family dines in the original du Pont Lodge restaurant.

Above: The du Pont Lodge's guest rooms were considered very nice and welcomed thousands of visitors after the lodge opened in the mid-1930s. Hotel accommodations were $1.50 and up, while cabins could be rented for $1.00 per day.

Left: The CCC's mission at Cumberland Falls included the clearing of trails, the building of roads and bridges and even the stringing of power lines. Two engineers survey for power line construction near the entrance to the park in this photograph dated December 1934.

Developing Kentucky's State Parks

As trees were cleared on trails, some were hewed for timber edging to stop erosion. CCC boys carried out this task manually, using axes and other hand tools, in December 1934 under the supervision of LEMs. In CCC photographs, LEMs can often be distinguished from CCC enrollees by their hats.

A newly cleared trail through one of the park's numerous pine groves led from SP-7 to the Moonbow Inn.

CCC enrollees used locally quarried stone to build steps on a roadside trail landscaped with Lespedeza to prevent erosion.

The CCC built a trail with a bridge that passed under Cumberland Falls. Visitors can no longer pass under the falls.

Developing Kentucky's State Parks

After a day's work, CCC enrollees loaded into trucks for the journey back to camp. This photograph is dated December 1934.

A young lady looks out at one of the scenic views from a newly constructed trail at Cumberland Falls. While not labeled, this photograph is believed to be one of a series taken by CCC photographer Anderson (first name unknown). A stylishly dressed young lady appears in many of Anderson's CCC photographs from Kentucky and Georgia.

Above: A CCC-constructed trailside log bench.

Left: The first CCC-constructed fire tower at Cumberland Falls State Park was located near Dryland Bridge and was constructed of vertical logs. It was replaced by the Pinnacle Knob Fire Tower in 1937.

Developing Kentucky's State Parks

In addition to du Pont Lodge, the CCC built fifteen rental cabins at Cumberland Falls. This was Cabin #11.

Group shelters of log and stone provided visitors with a place for family gatherings and picnics. This was a four-way shelter, as its interior was divided into four equal sections for four groups.

Trailside and overlook shelters like this six-sided one sheltered hikers during sudden inclement weather and often furnished visitors a scenic view during their respite.

Photographer Anderson again captured his companion outside the trailside shelter, where another type of trailside bench can be seen.

Above: Across the United States, the CCC constructed many buildings of local materials. In Kentucky, this was mostly limestone, sandstone and log topped with cedar or oak shake roofs. This large picnic or group shelter used all of those materials to create a structure befitting its rural surroundings.

Right: A safety sign painted by CCC technical staff and erected at the head of the company street urged the men to "Work Safe." Safety became a major concern of the corps after numerous accidents during the CCC's early days.

In 1924, Dr. Jillson also spoke of Natural Bridge:

Among the natural bridges of Kentucky there is one which because of its size and accessibility is of outstanding importance. This is the great rock arch located on the dividing ridge between Wolfe and Powell counties in the Red River Valley in central eastern Kentucky…The local station is Natural Bridge on the Louisville and Nashville Railroad. Because of its proximity to central Kentucky and its ease of approach it is yearly visited by thousands of tourists, many of whom are Kentuckians…Wind, frost and weather following in quick and helpful succession have served to widen the break in this old Coal Measure sandstone until today the arch is now high above the trail which leads up underneath it. The opening is 85 feet wide at the bottom. The bridge itself is 30 feet broad on top and is very strong and sound. It would easily support two heavily loaded railroad trains were it possible or advantageous to take them over it.

Yet Dr. Jillson was not the first to expound on the beauty and wonder of Natural Bridge. In 1889, Kentucky Union Railway executives recognized its potential and purchased the land around the sandstone arch. There, they built trails and a campground. The Louisville and Nashville Railroad later acquired the property, donating it to the state park system in 1926. Natural Bridge is one of Kentucky's four original state parks. In 1927, the newly constructed Hemlock Lodge opened on the original 1,137-acre park.

The CCC arrived at Natural Bridge in November 1934 and built SP-2, occupied by Company 567. The company's work consisted of the renovation of several park buildings, forest conservation and the construction of trails, shelters, latrines and cabins. SP-2 closed in the summer of 1936.

Established in 1924, Pine Mountain was Kentucky's first state park. Dr. Jillson, the newly appointed chairman of the park commission, first looked to Cumberland Gap. However, that area's potential to become a national park led Jillson to meet with a committed group of Bell County citizens interested in establishing a park near Pineville. First named Cumberland State Park, by 1938, the name had been changed to Pine Mountain to avoid confusion with Cumberland Falls and Cumberland Gap. Park facilities developed rapidly after the arrival of CCC Company 548 during the winter of 1933–34. SP-3 remained open until the summer of 1936. Company 563 joined the work in the summer of 1935 and remained at work until the CCC ended in 1942.

Kentucky established Levi Jackson Wilderness Road State Park on December 7, 1931, after the donation of 307 acres of land by descendants of Levi Jackson and John Freeman, the land's first white settlers. These two men

Developing Kentucky's State Parks

Above: Natural Bridge, created during the Paleozoic era, stands on a dividing ridge between Wolfe and Powell Counties and spans seventy-eight feet; it is sixty-five feet high. Trails lead to the top of the bridge, where visitors may enjoy a scenic vista of the surrounding countryside.

Right: Geologist F.C. Potter and Camp Superintendent R.H. Gunter examined the rock formation below the arch on July 31, 1935.

Above: Camp SP-2's personnel on July 31, 1935, included Company Clerk D.S. McElravey, Top Sergeant Elmer Mogoser, First Lieutenant B.F. Burdzinski, First Lieutenant M.E. Malkup, First Lieutenant R.B. Jeffrey and Educational Advisor John H. Martin.

Left: Richard E. Bishop visited the Natural Bridge CCC camp as the inspector for the Second District. He was the former superintendent at the camp. The photo's caption noted that he was "a man of keen insight, whose ideas on conservation and state parks are respected."

An early task of the enrollees was to clear dead chestnut trees on the trail to and directly below the bridge's arch.

In June 1934, the boys cleared undergrowth to reduce the danger of fire in the park. Many CCC men tell of being called out numerous times, even in the middle of the night, to fight forest fires. Forest fires were a frequent problem in the mid-1930s, as the Southeast and Midwest were experiencing a prolonged drought.

Biannual reports from each camp to CCC headquarters featured pages of photographs of the work. Some camp superintendents captured images of the men at work, such as this photo of Company 567 constructing a local road.

CCC enrollees learned carpentry skills while repairing the porch of the Hemlock Lodge. All of the porch's piers and exposed wood were rotted and deemed unsafe. The men removed this damaged wood and replaced it with native oak. This early Hemlock Lodge burned in the 1960s.

Above: Another
restoration project
centered on the
existing Victorian-era
refreshment stand.
While maintaining
its nineteenth-
century look, the
men replaced its
floor plates and lower
siding.

Right: Company 567
used this enclosed
dogtrot-style log
cabin as its recreation
hall. It existed on the
site long before the
CCC arrived.

Construction of one of the park's shelter houses began with heavy log beams.

The park superintendent captured the boys at work as the shelter progressed. Here, wood lathing was being attached so that a shingle roof could be applied.

Developing Kentucky's State Parks

In the summer of 1936, the CCC finished its work at Natural Bridge, leaving behind this log entrance station. The sign advertised the park's admission fee of ten cents. Today, none of Kentucky's state parks charges an entrance fee.

Chain Rock continues to be an attraction at Pine Mountain. The overhanging rock was first chained by local citizens in an effort to protect Pineville, which lies below. In 1933, the Pineville Chain Rock Club, assisted by the Boy Scouts and CCC, replaced the old chain. The new chain was 101 feet long, with seven-pound links.

CCC enrollees built many structures in the park. This handsome arched-stone fireplace graced the custodian's cottage.

While forestry work occupied many CCC man hours, the construction of forest and mountain trails consumed additional hours. In many areas, wood steps aided the hiker in attaining higher elevations within the park.

Developing Kentucky's State Parks

Stone, log and wood shingles cut on the park property created interesting structures, such as Pine Mountain's first entrance station.

The park offered camping, hiking, swimming and boating, along with its incredible mountain vistas. This CCC-built picnic shelter was a local gathering place on summer days.

The reflecting pool and stage at Pine Mountain's natural amphitheater in Laurel Cove is home to the park's Mountain Laurel Festival, now held the last weekend in May. CCC workers constructed the pool and stage so that the granite cliff serves as a backdrop to any performance.

established and ran a tavern along the Wilderness Road in Laurel County. The park also encompasses the site of one of early Kentucky's most tragic events, when twenty-four members of the McNitts party were massacred by Indians in 1786 on their way from Virginia to central Kentucky, and portions of Boone's Trace, Kentucky's other pioneer toll road.

CCC camp SP-5 housed Company 566. These men constructed cabins, footbridges, an observation tower and an auditorium and restored an old log house for the park's museum. Additionally, their tasks included forestry work and trail construction.

Northern Kentucky welcomed its first state park on August 12, 1931, when Butler Memorial Park was established. Now called General Butler State Park, the original three-hundred-acre tract composed part of William O. Butler's family farm. The park was a memorial to several generations of Butler family men who served their country in various wars. General Percival Butler served in the Revolutionary War before settling in Kentucky. William Orlando Butler, for whom the park is named, served in the War of 1812 and the Mexican War. Major Thomas Butler also served in the War of 1812 and was an aide to General Andrew Jackson at the Battle of New Orleans.

Nationwide, the CCC built approximately 3,116 fire or lookout towers, like this one at Levi Jackson. The scenic vista from the tower included all of the parklands and the mountains to the north.

Working to quarry local stone, CCC enrollees learned a valuable skill. Stone was quarried for structure and bridge foundations, as well as crushing for roadways. Levi Jackson's company mined this quarry.

After cutting the stone, the men placed it in the crusher and then loaded the crushed stone into trucks for transport to their current job site.

Using the quarried stone, the men built Levi Jackson's dam and, in so doing, created a wading pool.

Pride! Especially prevalent among the photographs sent to headquarters to document each camp's work were those that showed an individual or group of CCC men with their accomplishment, whether it was a simple log footbridge or a new picnic shelter.

At each park, the CCC was responsible for all of the infrastructure, as well the recreational venues and forestry or landscaping work. This bridge on the Daniel Boone trail was constructed of stone and logs.

Across the nation, some thirty-nine hundred historical structures were renovated for use in parks. The CCC restored this log cabin at Levi Jackson for use as the park's museum.

Developing Kentucky's State Parks

CCC workers surrounded the restored cabin with a rustic paling fence, planted trees and cleared debris from the area.

This old well sweep was restored by the enrollees. "Sweep" refers to the long pole that is lowered until the bucket goes down into the well, filling with water. The fulcrum is counterbalanced, making it easy to lift the bucket from the well. Yes, the man is posed on the wrong end of the sweep!

As parklands were created, it was often necessary to protect historical cemeteries. After clearing debris and undergrowth, the CCC built a stone wall to protect this family plot at Levi Jackson.

Hand tools and hard labor created a long day's work in the sun while the boys excavated Levi Jackson's lagoon.

Developing Kentucky's State Parks

On a cold day, dressed in their winter gear, the boys dug a water line.

The photographer captured Levi Jackson's completed administration building on a snowy winter's day.

At General Butler State Park, CCC photographer Anderson captured this view of the convergence of the Kentucky and Ohio Rivers from the park's Lookout Point, a rough stone tower built in irregular terraces by the CCC. Today, it is called Stone Overlook and is located on the park's Fossil Trail.

CCC men constructed a dam across the upper reaches of the valley to create this thirty-acre lake. Originally open for swimming, the lake is now used for boating (rowboats and paddle boats only) and fishing. The park's CCC-built stone visitor center can be seen behind the lake.

Developing Kentucky's State Parks

In 1935, the CCC reported the completion of trails, footbridges and landscaping throughout the park. Some thirty thousand native trees were planted, along with shrubbery where needed. This is another photograph taken by CCC photographer Anderson.

Each park developed an architectural style for its buildings. At General Butler, the buildings are mostly stacked stone, like this trailside shelter with fireplace. By 1935, the CCC had completed two shelter houses.

One significant task undertaken by the CCC was the restoration of Major Thomas L. Butler's 1859 residence. This Greek Revival residence was furnished in the style of the 1860s and was opened as a museum in the 1930s. It continues as a house museum today.

Working with stacked local stone and wood, CCC enrollees built small one- and two-room rental cabins at the park. In the 1930s, rental fees stood at two dollars per night for the furnished cabins.

At many parks across the nation, CCC men built "combination buildings." These centers often held the park's administrative office, as well as a small restaurant and a lobby for guests. Quite noticeable in this photo is the open shelter on the left end of Butler's headquarters.

Occupied by Company 592, SP-6 opened in early 1934 and closed in the winter of 1937–38. The CCC created a thirty-acre lake, constructed caretakers' cottages, rental cabins and shelter houses and restored an 1859-era Butler home.

Among the many photographic images stored at the National Archives, I found two pages of a report from Columbus-Belmont State Park illustrating a unique set of CCC activities accomplished by Company 583 at SP-8. The park was established on February 10, 1934, and the CCC arrived on July 17 of that year. Its role was the restoration of this Civil War battlefield's trenches and fortifications, an antebellum home that served as a Confederate hospital and visitor amenities. One of the park's feature elements was and is a sea anchor and chain used to bar the Mississippi River during the war. The photographs documented CCC workers building carriages for the park's cannons. Camp SP-8 closed during the winter of 1937–38.

In 1934, CCC Company 1540 began construction of cabins, gardens, shelter houses, trails and a museum at what was first named Audubon Memorial Museum, today's John James Audubon State Park. At the site of a

At Columbus-Belmont State Park, CCC boys built new carriages for old Civil War–era cannons. This photograph, dated March 15, 1937, shows one of the carriages before the cannon was mounted.

A subsequent photograph from the same report shows the cannon in place for loading on the carriage. This photograph was taken on March 23, 1937.

Developing Kentucky's State Parks

Using only manual labor, CCC boys loaded the heavy thirty-two-pounder, or Model 1829 cannon, onto the carriage on March 25, 1937. This cannon occupied a pivotal spot along the Mississippi River until a bank collapsed in 1942. The cannon and carriage fell into the Mississippi River and were not recovered for fifty-five years.

Another CCC task required the creation of a temporary furnace for heating traverse track. CCC enrollees bent the heated track to its required diameter by means of forms and jack screws. A portion of completed track can be seen on top of the forms. The use of traverse track allowed the permanently mounted gun to be pivoted for firing.

Blacksmithing skills used to construct a cannon carriage trunnion plate (a cylindrical projection on each side of a cannon, serving to support it on the cheeks of the carriage) were in little demand in the civilian market, but the general skills of ironworking and blacksmithing made these boys highly sought after when their enlistment time was over.

CCC enrollees make wood roofing shakes for the buildings at the future John James Audubon State Park. The boys are wearing slightly different versions of the denim work uniform. The two on the left have the most common version, with a vertical-opening slit pocket on each side.

A wood rail and post fence bordered the parade ground at Camp Cromwell, which housed Company 1540 at Audubon Park. Designated by an alphanumeric system, each camp also had a common name. Seldom do these names appear on official CCC documents.

mill once owned by Audubon, this park became a reality because of the hard work of local residents to secure 275 acres surrounding the mill site, as well as numerous Audubon artifacts. Only one CCC work-related photograph for this park was found, along with two similar images of the CCC camp.

Veteran and African American Camps

While much has been written about how the CCC enlisted boys and made them into men, little has been written in popular press about the presence of veterans and African Americans in the CCC. Both groups, however, were represented in the corps, along with Native Americans in many western states. Veterans came to the CCC in 1933, and African Americans were always included among the enrollees.

In 1932, President Hoover sent troops to push back, with tear gas, guns and bayonets, thousands of Spanish-American War and World War I veterans who marched on our Capitol, demanding early payment of their wartime service compensation pension, which was not due until 1945. FDR and Eleanor took a different approach when these desperate men marched again in early 1933. The new president and his wife welcomed the men with open arms, listened to their concerns and promised help to these "bonus army" men whose average age was forty and who were often impaired either in body or mental stability. These men were among the hardest hit by the Great Depression. It was said of the crisis that "Hoover sent the Army, Roosevelt sent his wife."

General Frank T. Hines, veterans administrator, came up with a solution in which he suggested the enlistment of willing veterans into the CCC as a way for many to receive hope as well as jobs. FDR listened and issued Executive Order No. 6129 to enroll twenty-five thousand war veterans into the CCC with no marital or age limitation. He offered every marcher in the bonus army immediate enlistment.

Over the next nine years, across the nation, some 225,000 veterans were housed in separate camps and carried out CCC projects suitable to their skills and physical condition. To many, the CCC became a source of redemption, where they could regain their place in society, earn a decent living and gain a skill. Many became career men of the CCC, as generous reenlistment provisions were granted. While bachelors were housed at the camp, many married men lived in nearby communities with their families and took only one or two daily meals at the camp.

In Kentucky, the CCC established a veteran company (1559) at F-1 in the Cumberland National Forest, near Pine Ridge, as one of its first camps in 1933. These veterans named their camp Peckerwood. Other veteran companies included PE-58, PE-59 and PE-60, also established in 1933. Veteran camps were mostly integrated, and no African American veteran camps were initially established in the state. Integrated camps usually listed approximately 75 to 95 percent white enrollees, with the remainder being listed as "colored." Within the camps, the enrollees lived in segregated facilities.

Veteran Company 1578 arrived at Cumberland Falls, SP-1, in July 1935. It worked to complete several projects begun by Company 509, including the du Pont Lodge. However, Company 1578 did not remain a veteran company and was reorganized as a junior company in 1936. It was later relocated to Tule Lake, California, and Merrill, Oregon.

At its opening, CCC enrollment officers were directed to enlist African Americans at the rate of 10 percent, which was roughly equal to their number in the national population. Although policy forbade discrimination, early efforts at CCC enlistment were not directed toward African Americans, especially in the South, where many qualified black applicants were purposely passed over. Those who managed to enlist faced hostile communities and the racist attitudes of their supervisors.

Early on, some camps were integrated; this was especially true in Kentucky. At integrated camps, black enrollees were assigned menial or subservient tasks, such as kitchen and latrine duty, and were denied the opportunities their white camp mates enjoyed. These young men were often quartered in a portion of the barracks separated by a wall and were forced to use the back door. In July 1935, Robert Fechner issued a directive ordering the complete segregation of "colored and white enrollees." However, official location and strength reports for Kentucky camps show that the practice of placing African Americans in each camp continued, especially at veteran camps.

In Kentucky, the CCC established only four segregated African American camps. SCS-2 at Russelville and SCS-25 at Sebree carried out soil conservation. At Mammoth Cave National Park, NP-1, Company 510 (one of four companies assigned to Mammoth Cave National Park) began as an integrated camp but was reorganized as a black camp and continued in existence until 1942. At Fort Knox, Army-2 opened in the summer of 1935 and closed in the summer of 1938.

Veteran and African American Camps

At Mammoth Cave, members of African American company 510 carried out all types of work associated with developing the national park. This segregated camp had its own library, where the men could spend their free time.

Camp Mammoth, home to Company 510, had a woodworking shop. Many camps taught woodworking, both as a job skill during the workday and as a recreational class during free time.

At Fort Knox, Army-2, Company 527, served as supply clerks for the CCC. These young men worked under the direction of an African American LEM to learn their job. At most African American camps, the army officers were white, with black educational advisors and LEMs being more common. *Courtesy of the Library of Congress.*

By 1936, the CCC had hired some black LEMs and educational advisors, yet camp management personnel remained largely white. The use of black officers at CCC camps was termed "experimental" by the army. Instead, the army insisted that only the "most carefully selected white officers" were assigned to "these colored camps."

When the Workday Ended

Many young CCC enrollees believed that life began at 4:30 p.m., when the workday ended. So it seemed to Ray Hoyt, author of *We Can Take It: A Short Story of the CCC*, first printed in 1935. His chapter on free time describes the numerous activities provided by the CCC camps for the men after the workday was completed. Not all of these activities were recreational, for almost immediately upon creation of the first CCC camps, the instructors and commanders realized that many of the young men were woefully undereducated. Three in every one hundred enrollees could not read or write.

In November 1934, President Roosevelt announced plans for a nationwide, Washington-directed CCC education service based on an ambitious plan submitted by W. Frank Person, the CCC director of selection. Each district would have a director of education who would hire teachers, see to construction of educational buildings at each camp and supply educational materials designed especially for the CCC. Local teachers were hired, and other classes were taught by the camp's army officers and LEMs. In June 1937, CCC statistics accounted for thirty-five thousand CCC men learning to read and write, while more than one thousand had received their high school diplomas. Additionally, at least twenty-six enrollees received college scholarships, and thirty-nine graduated from college.

At each camp, classes varied based on local opportunities. In some camps, local colleges and vocational schools worked with CCC leadership to offer a variety of educational programs. Generally, half of the classes were vocational and half educational. Educational classes were 16 percent elementary, 27 percent high school and 5 percent college.

Some enrollees engaged more in athletic pursuits than in educational ones. Opportunities varied again from camp to camp, but most camps had basketball, baseball and football teams and offered tennis, horseshoes, swimming, table tennis and boxing. Nearby camps often played one another

Morehead's Camp F-4 offered Company 578 a range of educational classes. Here, young men are participating in elementary classes. The female instructor was most likely one of the local teachers who worked at the camp after her regular school day was completed.

At Pikeville, CCC enrollees learned leather craft. This was camp P-81, occupied at various times by Companies 1577 and 1519.

When the Workday Ended

Although the photograph is labeled "Co. 3557 English class," the enrollees at the blackboard are working on math problems. Most likely, the class was for elementary students and combined subjects. At various times, Company 3557 was located at three different camps: Dawson Springs, Fort Knox and Otter Creek.

This tennis court may have been a bit rustic, but these two enrollees don't seem to care in this photograph taken on July 31, 1935, at Natural Bridge State Park's CCC camp.

On another court on that same day, some of the young men played a game of volleyball at a net strung in the area between the barracks at Natural Bridge.

Swimming Team #2 at Natural Bridge seems to have some very young members. I can only surmise they are the children of officers or LEMs at the camp.

When the Workday Ended

Fiddle making was not a skill taught at many CCC camps, yet it seems appropriate for Natural Bridge. This enrollee (name unknown) shows off his recently completed fiddle.

Paducah's Camp SCS-1, Company 3560, spent its workday building Noble Park and carrying out erosion and soil conservation methods. These four young men broadcasted a selection of vocal and instrumental music weekly on Paducah's WPAD.

Mammoth Cave's Company 582 sponsored the Mammoth Cave Serenaders. These Kentucky boys are Roy Riggs of Bonneville, Louis Calburn of Center, Cleatus Powers of Hampsville, Aaron Elder of Flint Springs and Thomas Baker of Beaver Dam (order unknown).

When the Workday Ended

Dawson Springs' Company 3557 photographed its baseball team in full uniform. Most teams had good equipment and uniforms. Proceeds from the camp's canteen, where Bull Durham tobacco and candy bars sold for four cents, were often used to purchase sporting equipment and uniforms.

At Morehead's Camp F-4, the young men could take a class in cooking and baking under the direction of Mr. G.P. Schmidt at the local college (now Morehead State University). This unit covered meat cutting.

In the Cumberland National Forest, Camp F-4 provided auto mechanics class for
Company 578.

Company 3557 moved quite often. Records place it at Fort Knox, Dawson Springs and Otter Creek near Rockhaven. While in this last location, some of the young men participated in a class in welding.

This comic from *Hysterical History: Civilian Conservation Corps* illustrates a CCC enrollee's view of a great free-time activity. *Author's personal collection.*

in organized events, and more often, the CCC teams played against local teams. Camps issued invitations for the locals to view the games. In exchange, local towns issued invitations to the CCC men for town dances, festivals and other athletic events.

Location and enrollees' interests influenced camp activities. For example, Camp Robinson's Company 547 enjoyed "a recreation hall with a piano, radio, pool tables, magazines, and the ever-waiting library." Camp libraries were issued a set number and selection of books that were rotated from camp to camp. This selection of books included: adventure and mystery (seventeen), miscellaneous fiction (twenty-nine), westerns (twelve), travel (twenty), history and biography (twelve), science fiction (twenty-nine), athletics (five) and religion (three), along with forty-five periodicals and the Sears-Roebuck catalog. Newspapers and magazines stayed at the camp and were among the most frequently read.

Religious activities were limited at some camps located far from towns and villages, but most camps provided transportation to local churches on Sunday mornings. Others held services at the camp. Carmen W. Elliott of Company 547 revealed in their company log that Protestant ministers from nearby Jackson held Sunday services at the camp, and the Catholic boys could attend Mass every other Sunday in nearby Hazard.

One CCC Man

Attending a reunion of CCC enrollees in 2009 leaves one indelible impression: these men are rapidly dwindling in number each year. Now in their late seventies to nineties, few of these men are left to tell their stories. Some leave behind photographic collections, passed down to their children and grandchildren, that illustrate their CCC stories. These personal collections can often divulge a forgotten snippet of America's past. Presented here are photos and anecdotes from one such collection.

Fred Jerome Powers, son of Dent and Susie Minerva (Evans) Powers of Albany, Indiana, joined the CCC in 1934. He was nineteen years old and was the oldest of nine children. His initial conditioning training took place at Fort Knox in Company J-57, after which he was assigned to Company 592 at General Butler State Park. Many of this company were Indiana boys and are fondly remembered by older residents of Carrollton today; especially since some of these young men married local girls and remained in Kentucky.

Fred served as a cook and was promoted to chief cook for the company. Fred met and eloped with Mildred Hendricks, a Carrollton girl, on February 8, 1936, while still enlisted in the CCC. He was removed from his position as chief cook but served out the remainder of his enlistment period. Fred and Mildred were forced to live on his five dollars per month until Fred's enlistment period ended. During Fred's CCC days, he lost his father, a brother and two sisters to tuberculosis.

During World War II, Fred Powers worked as a security guard at the Jeffersontown Proving Grounds in Charleston, Indiana, where artillery shells were made and tested. After the war, he returned to Kentucky and worked for Kentucky Utilities until his retirement in 1981. Fred died on January 11, 2004.

CCC Company J-57 posed for its graduation photo at Fort Knox with Captain E.S. Vannier and Sergeant P. Lawrence. *Courtesy of Fred Powers's family.*

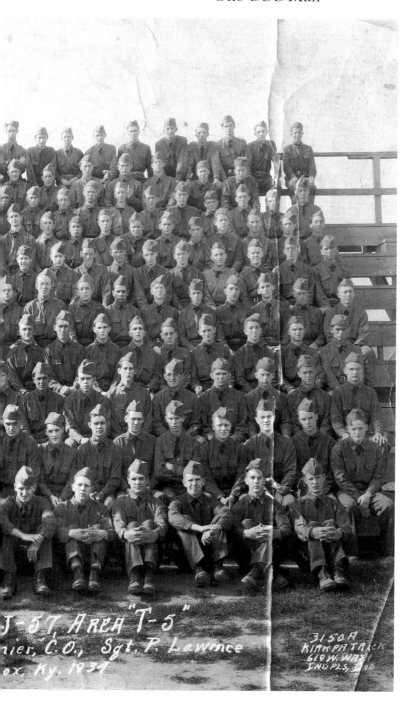

Fred sent quite a few postcards home that featured the CCC camp at General Butler. On the back, Fred wrote, "These are some pictures I bought taken of the camp it will give you some idea of the place down here." *Courtesy of Fred Powers's family.*

Fred's collection of images includes this one of shirtless CCC boys constructing the "lookout tower." *Courtesy of Fred Powers's family.*

One CCC Man

Fred Powers served as a company cook at General Butler State Park. Pictured are cooks Krutz, Powers and Kong, according to Fred's caption. *Courtesy of Fred Powers's family.*

Leisure time included going with the gang to the now completed lookout. Fred's caption reads, "Koolie, Midge, Fred, _____, Louise, Eddie, Bessie, Brownie, Bobs." *Courtesy of Fred Powers's family.*

Fred played catcher on Company 592's baseball team, pictured here in 1934. He is second from the right in the back row. *Courtesy of Fred Powers's family.*

One CCC Man

Fred posed with Mildred Hendricks of Carrollton, the local girl he married. They had two sons and two daughters. Many years later, Fred and Mildred were members of the Butler Generals Square Dancing Club. *Courtesy of Fred Powers's family.*

Posing for the camera, Fritz (left), Jimmie "Red" Myers and Fred sit on the steps of one of the CCC buildings. *Courtesy of Fred Powers's family.*

The Flood of 1937

Black Sunday, January 24, 1937, followed twenty-seven days of rain in Tennessee, Kentucky, Indiana, Illinois and Ohio. Creeks and tributaries in the Cumberland, Tennessee, Ohio and Mississippi river basins reached flood levels never before recorded. The rivers began rising to dangerous levels on the seventeenth, and by the twenty-fourth, thousands of acres along these rivers were inundated with near freezing water. On the Ohio, Black Sunday witnessed record levels of over 80.0 feet above flood level at Louisville and 60.8 feet above flood level at Paducah on February 2. Many buildings in downtown Paducah still bear plaques showing the flood's high-water mark.

Residents along the rivers had suffered through previous floods; the most recent and deadly in 1884 had seen the Ohio 46.7 feet above flood level. In 1937, the Ohio stayed above flood level for eighteen consecutive days. In Louisville, alone, thirty-four thousand homes were flooded, while 70 percent of the town's residents were evacuated for over three weeks. Smaller towns and communities along the river suffered even greater consequences, for along with the rising waters came a cold snap that left over 20.0 feet of ice in some communities. Towns like Birmingham, which sat directly on the Tennessee River in Marshall County, suffered some of the worst devastation due to their proximity to the rising waters. Many homes had floodwaters in their second stories. Schools and hospitals were destroyed. It has been estimated that 270,000 people were left homeless after the flood and that Kentucky suffered over $200 million in damage to public and private property. The flood's death toll approached 500 persons and countless head of livestock.

Thousands of people were housed in shelters along the rivers. Food, heat and drinking water were in short supply. FDR declared a national emergency, and all possible agencies were called in to help. FDR

CCC Company 1562, using boats of all types, rescued over two hundred families near its camp (SCS-15) at Madisonville. This photograph shows the company's veteran enrollees rescuing a family and some of their possessions near the junction of the Pond and Green Rivers near Ashbyburg, Kentucky, at the height of the flood. Company 1562 also rescued hundreds of head of livestock from inundated farms.

Along the rivers, CCC camps also distributed food to thousands of families. Here, CCC boys are stocking bags of food to be delivered to shelters, churches, schools and homes where people were housed during the flood.

Many CCC camps became shelters and housed refugees in their barracks and other buildings. This photograph, taken in a CCC kitchen, shows rescued victims "turning in, with good spirit, to peel *spuds* for the several hundred people housed at the camp." The camp's name was not given in this press photograph released by the CCC.

Next page, top: Simply entitled "Refugee Children in Barracks," this photograph illustrates how the flooding affected all age groups and shows how the children coped with the disaster.

Next page, bottom: African American CCC enrollees lived in a steel barge on the Mississippi River while working on the levee near Hickman, Kentucky. The CCC company was not identified.

Another CCC company was housed in Hickman's Masonic Lodge while battling the floodwaters. This may be Company 1474 from Camp Montgomery in Clarksville, Tennessee.

Next page, top: Company 3363 from SCS-18 at Carlisle helped clean up Maysville, Kentucky, after the Ohio River floodwaters began receding.

Next page, bottom: Company 3363 worked in shifts during and after the flood. Here, its men are shown loading up for the return to camp after completing their work shift in Maysville.

The Flood of 1937

In Maysville, CCC enrollees trucked flood debris to a landfill near town.

instructed CCC companies to "build levees, police flooded areas, and evacuate refugees." In Kentucky, the CCC reacted by sending whole companies into remote towns and villages along the rivers to provide assistance.

In Paducah, Company 3560 set up a field kitchen at the end of Broadway and Avendale Heights, where the now closed Coca-Cola bottling plant stands. Estimates put the number fed at about eight thousand per day, while the water rose to within fifty feet of the temporary kitchen. Other members of the company picked up "water refugees" and brought them to safety or filled sandbags along the river. The CCC camp at Paducah was underwater during the flood.

After the flood of 1937, the Tennessee Valley Authority began work on a massive dam at Gilbertsville, Kentucky. Engineers positioned the dam on the river so as to provide as much relief as possible from future catastrophic floods. The CCC played a minor role in this project. In the

Identified simply as CCC laborers from Unit B at Jonathan Creek, May 16, 1941, this photo shows the young men who excavated an archaeological site and uncovered remains of eighty-nine house structures and eight stockade lines from the site's Native American occupation. Work was never completed, as fieldwork was prematurely terminated on March 20, 1942, when the laborers and site supervisors were mobilized for World War II. *Courtesy of the William S. Webb Museum of Anthropology, University of Kentucky.*

Archaeologists most often photograph excavations without any of the workers present. This is one of only a few photographs from the Jonathan Creek site that shows the CCC boys at work. They were excavating Feature 27, the stockade line in Unit B. *Courtesy of the William S. Webb Museum of Anthropology, University of Kentucky.*

fall of 1940, CCC Company 536 was established at Camp TVA-P-1. Its work was quite different from other camps, as the men were employed in emergency archaeological excavations at the Jonathan Creek site. The boys worked under the direction of archaeologists from the University of Kentucky and TVA archaeologist Charles G. Wilder to excavate burials and archaeological artifacts from the Jonathan Creek site, a Mississippian-period Native American village. Archaeologists recorded six earthen mounds and discovered evidence of the site's stockade during the excavations.

The Lasting Legacy of the CCC

As early as June 1935, newspapers extolled the virtues of the CCC. The *Cincinnati Enquirer* published a piece stating:

> *Most popular of all the New Deal ideas is that of the Civilian Conservation Corps. One reason for this is that it had so few brass ornaments. It is a relief plan but not on an extravagant scale…This plan has saved many a young man from being a tramp…If all other New Deal programs were as good as is the Civilian Conservation Corps the country would have reason to rejoice, for it is a success.*

In October 1935, *Mountain Life and Work* printed an article about the CCC that first stressed the financial benefits of the CCC in Kentucky's mountainous regions. In the development of commercial forestry, the CCC created permanent jobs for game wardens, fish wardens and workers in mills and other processing plants. By building parks, revenue from tourists could be anticipated and would be a sustainable resource. However, Nat Frame's real emphasis was on the CCC's "great advantage to the man in the camp." Frame insisted that it was the *man* who was being conserved in eastern Kentucky's twenty-seven CCC camps as he learned health and sanitation, was "governed by a regular and disciplined camp routine" and was given "honest-to-goodness constructive work," along with vocational instruction, an education and recreation. He cited a young CCC enrollee who believed the corps brought out the "best in our young men."

Another firsthand story about the importance of the CCC was located among official CCC documents. The document is a letter from a former CCC enrollee to F. Marion Rust, camp superintendent, at Columbus-Belmont State Park. It demonstrates that even in 1936, one young man realized the impact the CCC had on his life and took time to put words to paper. From Cleveland, Ohio, he wrote:

Dear Mr. Rust,

My departure from Kentucky has but been a mere month ago and I feel it my duty to write you this letter while my memory of Columbus and the Belmont-Columbus Park are yet still fresh in my mind.

In all my twenty years of life I cannot recall ever having enjoyed it as much as when I spent those memorable days working in that part of the country.

Under your guidance and your leadership it was an extreme pleasure to work. It seemed to stimulate the boys to hear you speak at those Wednesday Safety meetings. It sure raised the morality of the boys.

One cannot but help to enjoy walking through what was nothing more than a large area of corn fields and wild brush and huge wash-outs eighteen months ago and see the improvements to date and marvel at the progress in so little a time.

The knowledge I gained while an enrollee shall be of value to me some day. I have gained much and lost little.

If there was the slightest chance of getting back at Columbus, I would enlist immediately. That's how much I liked it!

Very truly Yours,

Herman "Hitler" Lear

Generally, the CCC developed a well-rounded man who worked, played and learned with equal enthusiasm. Listening to oral histories collected by the Kentucky Historical Society and attending reunions of former CCC men, one gains an immediate appreciation for who these men were when they joined the CCC and who they became. Most joined out of necessity—their families desperately needed the twenty-five dollars per month that they would be sending home. When asked what his mother said when he enlisted, one enrollee replied, "Goodbye." His explanation revealed how his mother would now have one less mouth to feed, one less child to worry about each day and understood that his sacrifice would provide for all of those at home.

Yet these were young men who had, in most cases, never traveled farther from home than their local communities. Most had never lived anywhere but home. They arrived anxious and scared. They depended on the mail for news of their family. If an enrollee's home was nearby, he might see his family on weekends; otherwise, he was restricted to a short visit at the end of his six month's enlistment period if he reenlisted for another six months. Few CCC enrollees left after only one enlistment period.

Using only official records, it is burdensome to trace company histories, especially since companies moved from camp to camp as needed. The

The Lasting Legacy of the CCC

Labeled "Letter from Home," this unsigned sketch illustrates the loneliness and separation felt by many CCC boys. Fred Powers, on one postcard sent home right after his arrival at General Butler State Park, wrote, "I've expected to hear from you every day but haven't as yet. If something is wrong let me know."

Someone captured a view of General Butler's CCC camp in the background while photographing "Crockett, Tuttles, and Fred." *Courtesy of Fred Powers's family.*

most accurate record of company movements appears to be CCC annuals produced for each district each year. These books are now difficult to locate but are a wealth of information and photographs about the individual companies. Personal CCC stories are to be found in recorded interviews made at reunions, in a few written histories and, most often, in captions on photographs. These personal photographs most often show the camp only as a backdrop for a group of CCC friends or the LEMs who provided guidance and training to the boys. Occasionally, a visitor to the camp would be captured by the camera lens.

Often taken on the work site, photographs of LEMs provide some insight into those respected by the company. Fred Powers photographed "Langford and O'Leary" at General Butler State Park. *Courtesy of Fred Powers's family.*

Entitled simply "State Foreman Perry and Kinslow," this photograph captures a scenic view at General Butler State Park. From an additional photograph in the collection, State Foreman Sam Perry can be identified as the man on the right. *Courtesy of Fred Powers's family.*

Fred Powers photographed the "old tree gang" at lunch with their mess kits in hand but cut off the heads of the men in the back. Being the company cook, Fred probably only visited the work sites when delivering the noon meal. Each man was responsible for carrying his own mess kit to the work site. *Courtesy of Fred Powers's family.*

The Lasting Legacy of the CCC

Thomas Rost Jr. sketched CCC enrollees loading the trucks for travel to the day's work site. The newspaper *Happy Days* and several books published at that time used drawings such as this one to illustrate daily life in the "three Cs."

This poem, accompanied by an appropriate illustration, appeared in *Hysterical History: Civilian Conservation Corps. Author's personal collection.*

In Kentucky, some 89,500 young men participated in the CCC. Most enlisted for more than one six-month period. It has been estimated that over 150 types of jobs were performed by the CCC. Corps training and discipline provided a substantial advantage when many were drafted and mobilized at the beginning of World War II. These men gained an understanding of life, a chance to travel and meet new people, a sense of independence and an education and vocational training. Mostly, they learned to be men, with their heads held high, who recognized that they had been entrusted with a chore that would benefit their nation and that they had preformed it well. FDR gave them a sense of pride in their accomplishments and themselves.

The official seal of the Civilian Conservation Corps.

APPENDIX A
Soil Conservation and Other Camps

TABLE 1. SOIL CONSERVATION CAMPS

CAMP	COMP.	COUNTY	PO	DATES ACTIVE
SCS1	3560	McCracken	Paducah	Summer '35–Summer '42
SCS2	3562	Logan	Russelville	Summer '35–Summer '42
SCS3	unknown	Ohio	Hartford	Summer '35–Winter '38/'39
SCS4	566	Shelby	Shelbyville	Summer '35–Summer '39
SCS5	3541	Boone	Walton	Summer '35–Summer '42
SCS 6/ACSA 1	1562	Union	Morganfield	Summer '35–Summer '42
PE 56/SCS 7	1534	Hickman	Clinton	Summer '33–Winter '37/'38
PE 57/SCS 8	508	Marshall	Benton	Summer '33–Summer '36
PE 59/SCS 9	1542	Crittenden	Marion	Summer '33–Summer '36
PE 60/SCS 10	1550	Webster	Dixon	Summer '33–Winter '37/'38
PE 63/SCS 11	1516	Breckinridge	Hardinsburg	Summer '33–Summer '36
PE 66/SCS 12	1515	Hardin	Elizabethtown	Winter '33/'34–Summer '40
PE 67/SCS 13	599	Trigg	Cadiz	Winter '33/'34–Summer '39
PE 68/SCS 14	1527	Calloway	Murray	Winter '33/'34–Summer '39
PE 69/SCS 15	1562	Hopkins	Madisonville	Summer '34–Winter '37/'38
SCS 16	3559	Graves	Mayfield	Summer '35–Summer '42
SCS 17	unknown	Campbell	Alexandria	Summer '35–Summer '36
SCS 18	3563	Nicholas	Carlisle	Summer '35–Summer '41
SCS 21	599	Caldwell	Princeton	Summer '39–Summer '42

CAMP	COMP.	COUNTY	PO	DATES ACTIVE
SCS 22	unknown	Boyle	Danville	Summer '35–Summer '42
SCS 23	1577	Grayson	Leitchfield	Summer '35–Winter '41/'42
SCS 24	3554	Daviess	Owensboro	Winter '39/'40–Winter '41/'42
SCS 25	527	Webster	Sebree	Winter '39/'40–Summer '41
SCS 26	1515	Scott	Georgetown	Summer '40–Summer '42
SCS 27	1562	Fleming	Flemingsburg	Summer '40–Summer '42

SCS: Soil Conservation Service
ACSA: no description in official papers
PE: private erosion

TABLE 2. OTHER CAMPS ON STATE AND PRIVATE LANDS

CAMP	COMPANY	COUNTY	POST OFFICE	DATES ACTIVE
S-51	547	Breathitt	Noble	Summer '33–Summer '36
P-52	598	Whitley	Emlyn	Summer '33–Summer '36
S-53	512	Harlan	Putney	Summer '33–Summer '39
P-54	1529	Leslie	Wooton	Summer '33–Summer '36
P-55	1518	Martin/Lawrence	Richardson	Summer '33–Winter '34/'35
PE-58	1562	Hopkins	Dawson Springs	Summer '33–Summer '34
PE-61	1515	Muhlenberg	Central City	Summer '33–Summer '34
PE-62	1517	Ohio	Hartford	Summer '33–Summer '34
P-64	555	Harlan	Cumberland	Summer '33–Winter '37/'38
P-65	597	McCreary	Steans	Summer '33–Summer '36
P-73	1518	Johnson	Paintsville	Winter '34/'35–Summer '39
P-74	3545	Harlan	Alva/Pathfork	Summer '35–Winter '39/'40
P-75	3536	Harlan	Evarts	Summer '35–Winter '37/'38
P-76	3548	Perry	Buckhorn	Summer '35–Winter '37/'38
P-77	3535	Leslie	Bledsoe	Summer '35–Summer '41
P-80	3530/3563	Clay	Manchester/Gooscrock	Summer '35–Summer '42
P-81	1577/1519	Pike	Pikeville/Nigh	Summer '35–Summer '41
S-82	1518	Pike/Letcher	Hellier	Summer '39–Summer '42

Soil Conservation and Other Camps

CAMP	COMPANY	COUNTY	POST OFFICE	DATES ACTIVE
P-83	512	Leslie	Chappell	Summer '39–Summer '42
S-84	3545	Harlan	Crummies	Winter '39/'40–Summer '42
D-1	3554	Daviess	Owensboro	Summer '35–Winter '39/'40
D-2	3561	Webster	Sebree	Summer '35–Winter '39/'40

P: private
S: state
PE: private erosion
D: drainage

TABLE 3. OTHER CAMPS

CAMP	COMP.	NAME	COUNTY	PO	DATES ACTIVE
NP-1	510	Mammoth Cave	Edmondson	Cave City	Summer '33–Winter '41/'42
NP-2	543	Mammoth Cave	Edmondson	Cave City	Winter '33/'34–Summer '42
NP-3	582	Mammoth Cave	Edmondson	Cave City	Summer '34–Winter '37/'38
NP-4	516	Mammoth Cave	Edmondson	Cave City	Summer '34–Summer '42
NP-5	3557	Otter Creek	Meade	Rock Haven	Winter '39/'40–Summer '41
Army-1/ NP(D)-1	527/3554	Fort Knox	Hardin	Fort Knox	Summer '35–Summer '36
Army-2	527	Fort Knox	Hardin	Fort Knox	Summer '35–Summer '38
Army-3	unknown	Fort Knox	Hardin	Fort Knox	Summer '35–Summer '36
TVA-P-1	536	Jonathan Creek	Marshall	Benton	Summer '40–Summer '42
NP(C)-2	3557	Fort Knox	Meade	West Point	Summer '41–Summer '42

Mammoth Cave

The National Park Service established four CCC camps to work on the development of Mammoth Cave National Park, including the first in Kentucky. Called Camp 1, the CCC constructed this camp on the site of the former Bluegrass Country Club. The four CCC companies undertook the massive job of creating trails, both above- and underground; building park structures and roads; clearing landscape; planting trees; and installing modern utilities in the park. At that time, Mammoth Cave was a local attraction, although it had been authorized as a national park in 1926, and the plan was for the CCC to provide the labor while national park personnel developed the park's infrastructure.

As early as July 28, 1935, the *New York Times* was declaring that "CCC Workers Take Hazards Out of a Trip Into Its Fantastic Caverns by Building Safe Walks." The article discussed a new sanded trail, taking eight hours to traverse, that was built by CCC boys using pick axes, shovels and wheelbarrows. This trail included a stop at the "Snowball Dining Room," approximately midway on the tour, where hot lunches were served. Even as this announcement was being made, the CCC was busy working on another route within the cave.

Three of Mammoth Cave's CCC companies were white and the other was African American (NP-1). The camps had segregated barracks, mess halls and educational buildings and rarely worked together on work projects. However, the camps did share a recreation building, which they named "Whoopie House."

Camp NP-1 is credited with much of the work inside the cave, clearing trails, building bridges and stairs and making the cave safe for visitors. In 1940, Acting Superintendent R. Taylor Hoskins wrote that enrollees had spent twelve-thousand man days on cave improvements totaling twenty-four miles of trails. The other three camps worked aboveground, clearing old structures, building new park structures, creating fifty-three miles of graveled roads and planting over 750,000 trees. They also built picnic areas and fire towers, laid sewer and water lines and strung telephone wires.

Work at the park was completed in 1941, but America's entry into World War II postponed the park's dedication until September 1946. A fascinating and comprehensive collection of photographs of CCC work at Mammoth Cave is held by Western Kentucky University and can be seen online at www.wku.edu/Library/nps/ccc/index.html.

Sources

Camp Robinson Log. "Company 547 of the Civilian Conservation Corps in Breathitt County at Noble, Kentucky, 1933–34." http://digilab.browardlibrary. org/cdm4/document.php?CISOROOT=/ccc&CISOPTR=2485&REC=1.

Cohen, Stan. *The Tree Army: A Pictorial History of the Civilian Conservation Corps, 1933–1942.* Missoula, MT: Pictorial Histories Publishing Company, 1980.

Darnell, Mrs. James. *Biennial Report of the Kentucky State Park Commission: January 1, 1929–December 31, 1931.*

Dearborn, Ned H. *Once In a Lifetime: A Guide to the CCC Camp.* New York: Charles E. Merrill Company, 1936.

Frame, Nat T. "Kentucky Mountain Boys in the CCC." *Mountain Life and Work* (October 1935).

Hoyt, Ray. *"We Can Take It": A Short Story of the CCC.* New York: American Book Company, 1935.

———. *"Your CCC": A Handbook for Enrollees.* Second edition. Washington, D.C.: Happy Days Publishing Co., Inc., n.d.

Jillson, Willard Roose. *Kentucky State Parks.* Kentucky Geological Survey, 1927.

Merrill, Perry H. *Roosevelt's Forest Army: A History of the Civilian Conservation Corps 1933–1942.* N.p.: Perry H. Merrill, 1981.

"New Deal for Parks: Civilian Conservation Corps Celebrates Its 75th Anniversary." *Uncommon Ground* 13, no. 2 (Summer 2008).

Paige, John C. *The Civilian Conservation Corps and the National Park Service, 1933–1944: An Administrative History.* N.p.: National Park Service, Department of the Interior, 1985.

Salmond, John A. *The Civilian Conservation Corps, 1933–1942.* Durham, NC: Duke University Press, 1967.

Schroeder, Sissel. "Reclaiming New Deal–Era Civic Archaeology: Exploring the Legacy of William S. Webb and the Jonathan Creek Site." *CRM: The Journal of Heritage Stewardship* 2, no. 1 (Winter 2005).

Visit us at
www.historypress.net